D1622520

BASKETBALL'S
GREATEST
STARS

KYRIE IRVING

by Matt Tustison

SportsZone

An Imprint of Abdo Publishing
abdopublishing.com

SOMERSET CO. LIBRARY
BRIDGEWATER, N.J. 08807

abdopublishing.com

Published by Abdo Publishing, a division of ABDO, PO Box 398166, Minneapolis, Minnesota 55439. Copyright © 2017 by Abdo Consulting Group, Inc. International copyrights reserved in all countries. No part of this book may be reproduced in any form without written permission from the publisher. SportsZone™ is a trademark and logo of Abdo Publishing.

Printed in the United States of America, North Mankato, Minnesota
092016
012017

THIS BOOK CONTAINS
RECYCLED MATERIALS

Cover Photos: Carlos Osorio/AP Images, foreground; Ron Schwane/AP Images, background
Interior Photos: Carlos Osorio/AP Images, 1 (foreground); Ron Schwane/AP Images, 1 (background); Marcio Jose Sanchez/AP Images, 4-5, 7; Eric Risberg/AP Images, 6, 27; Rick Bowmer/AP Images, 8; Scott Stewart/AP Images, 9; Gerry Broome/AP Images, 10-11, 14-15; Jim Rinaldi/Icon SMI 154/Newscom, 12, 13; Bill Kostroun/AP Images, 16-17; Amy Sancetta/AP Images, 18; Mark Duncan/AP Images, 19, 22, 24-25; Eric Gay/AP Images, 20-21, 26, 28-29; Gerald Herbert/AP Images, 23

Editor: Todd Kortemeier
Series Designer: Laura Polzin

Publisher's Cataloging-in-Publication Data
Names: Tustison, Matt, author.
Title: Kyrie Irving / by Matt Tustison.
Description: Minneapolis, MN : Abdo Publishing, 2017. | Series: Basketball's
    greatest stars | Includes index.
Identifiers: LCCN 2016945488 | ISBN 9781680785463 (lib. bdg.) |
    ISBN 9781680798098 (ebook)
Subjects: LCSH: Irving, Kyrie, 1992- --Juvenile literature. | Basketball players--
    Australia--Biography--Juvenile literature.
Classification: DDC 796.323 [B]--dc23
LC record available at http://lccn.loc.gov/2016945488

CONTENTS

SHOT AT A TITLE

It was a game-winner. A series-winner. A championship-winner. Kyrie Irving hit the biggest shot in Cleveland Cavaliers history.

The Cavaliers and Golden State Warriors were tied 89-89. It was the final minute of Game 7 of the 2016 National Basketball Association (NBA) Finals in Oakland. Irving got the ball. He dribbled around the perimeter. He stepped back and released a three-pointer. He nailed it with 53 seconds to go.

FAST FACT

Irving averaged 27.1 points per game in the 2016 Finals.

Kyrie Irving and the Cavaliers had to stay focused in Game 7 of the 2016 NBA Finals.

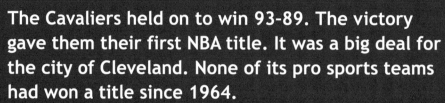

The Cavaliers held on to win 93-89. The victory gave them their first NBA title. It was a big deal for the city of Cleveland. None of its pro sports teams had won a title since 1964.

A downtown parade a few days later honored the Cavs. Irving and teammate LeBron James rode in style in fancy cars. Fans lined the streets to celebrate with their heroes.

Irving hugs teammate LeBron James, 23, after winning the NBA title.

Irving was all smiles after becoming a first-time NBA champion.

FAST FACT

One year earlier, Irving was injured in Game 1 of the Finals. He missed the rest of the series.

THE EARLY YEARS

Kyrie Irving was born on March 23, 1992 in Melbourne, Australia. His dad, Drederick, is from the United States. But he moved to Australia to play basketball.

Kyrie did not live there long. His family moved to New Jersey when he was two years old.

Irving, *left*, goes for a loose ball playing with Team USA as a high school senior in 2010.

Drederick Irving, *left*, played college basketball at Boston University but didn't make it to the NBA.

FAST FACT

Irving is a citizen of both Australia and the United States.

FAST FACT

Kyrie played a game at the home arena of the New Jersey Nets in fourth grade. He wanted to play in the NBA from that time on.

Two years later, Kyrie's mother, Elizabeth, died suddenly from an infection. To honor her memory, he has a tattoo of her name over his heart. Kyrie has a sister, Asia, and a half-sister, London. Drederick raised them with the help of Kyrie's aunts.

Kyrie knew he wanted to be a basketball player. When he was in fourth grade, he made a promise to himself. He wrote on the wall in his bedroom closet that he was going to make it to the NBA. He even underlined it three times.

Irving became a highly recruited player by the time he got to high school.

HIGH SCHOOL AND COLLEGE

Kyrie started high school at Montclair Kimberley Academy in Montclair, New Jersey. He led them to a state basketball title when he was a sophomore.

Kyrie went to St. Patrick High School in Elizabeth, New Jersey for his last two years. He had grown to 6 feet 2 inches (1.9 meters) tall. He was ranked among the best point guards in the country.

As a senior, Irving played in the McDonald's All American Game for the best high school players in the country.

Irving goes up for a dunk in the All American Game.

FAST FACT

Irving's motto is "Hungry and Humble." He used to write it on his gym bag in school.

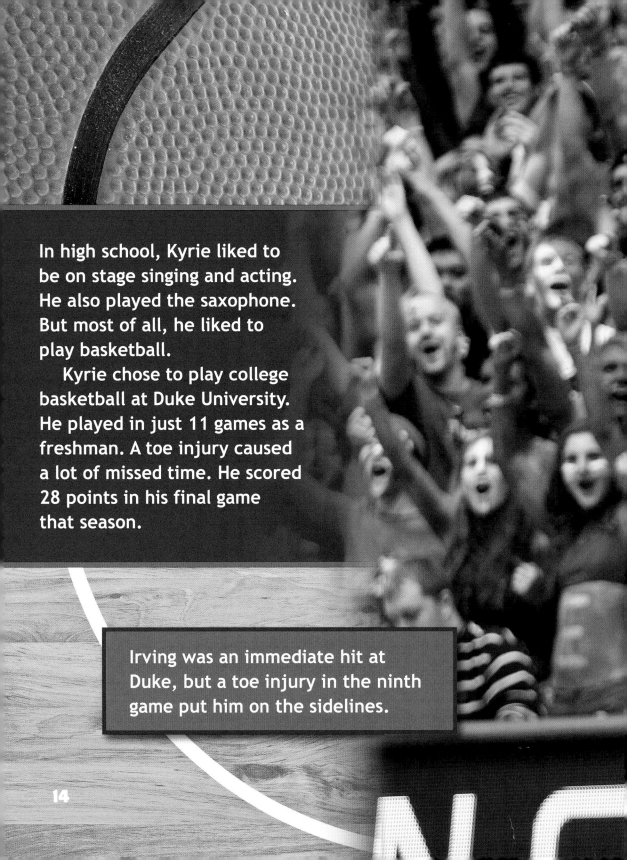

In high school, Kyrie liked to be on stage singing and acting. He also played the saxophone. But most of all, he liked to play basketball.

Kyrie chose to play college basketball at Duke University. He played in just 11 games as a freshman. A toe injury caused a lot of missed time. He scored 28 points in his final game that season.

Irving was an immediate hit at Duke, but a toe injury in the ninth game put him on the sidelines.

FAST FACT

Irving left Duke after just one season. But he promised his father that he would someday earn his college degree.

MAKING IT IN THE NBA

NBA teams had only 11 college games to watch to evaluate Irving. But they liked what they saw. Cleveland selected him first overall in the 2011 NBA Draft.

He quickly showed he was ready. Irving played in the Rising Stars Challenge in 2012. The game features the NBA's best first- and second-year players. Irving dominated. He hit all eight three-pointers he took. He finished with 34 points.

Irving takes the stage with NBA Commissioner David Stern after being drafted by Cleveland.

FAST FACT

Cleveland also chose
Tristan Thompson in the
2011 draft. Thompson
and Irving had played
against each other
in high school.

The Cavs won just 21 games in Irving's rookie season, but Irving played a big role. He hit game-winning baskets in three Cleveland wins.

Irving averaged more than 18 points, five assists, and one steal per game. He made more than 45 percent of his shots from the field. Only five other NBA rookies had ever hit those numbers. Irving was named NBA Rookie of the Year.

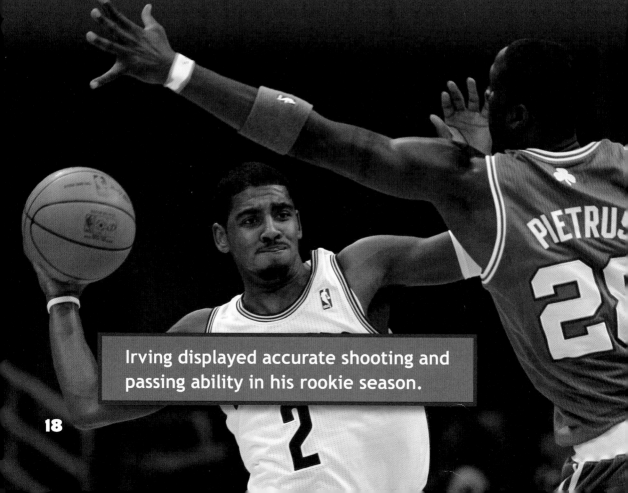

Irving displayed accurate shooting and passing ability in his rookie season.

Irving smiles as he receives the 2012 NBA Rookie of the Year Award.

GAINING EXPERIENCE

Irving continued to play well in his second NBA season. In February 2013, he starred at All-Star weekend in Houston. Irving scored 32 points in the Rising Stars Challenge. He then won the Three-Point Shootout.

Then came his first All-Star Game. He had 15 points and four assists. Irving's layup in the fourth quarter pulled the East to within five points. But the West held on to win 136-126.

Irving goes up for a dunk in the 2013 NBA All-Star Game.

FAST FACT

In December 2012, Irving scored 41 points in a loss to New York. At age 20, he became the youngest NBA player to score 40 or more points in Madison Square Garden.

Irving had become an elite player. But the Cavaliers struggled again. They finished the 2012-13 season 24-58. The next year, fans voted Irving to start the 2014 All-Star Game in New Orleans.

Irving had 31 points and 14 assists. He won the game's Most Valuable Player (MVP) award. And the Cavaliers improved a little, finishing 33-49.

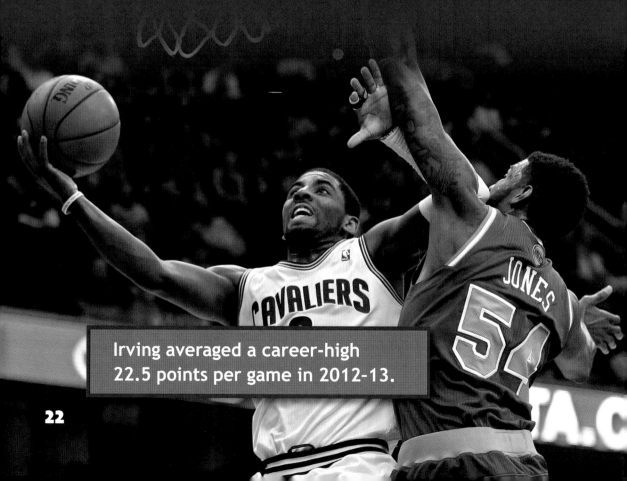

Irving averaged a career-high 22.5 points per game in 2012-13.

Irving holds up his MVP trophy after the 2014 All-Star Game.

FAST FACT

In April 2014, Irving set a career high with 44 points in a loss to the Charlotte Bobcats.

THE BIG THREE

In the summer of 2014, everything changed for Irving and the Cavaliers. Ohio native LeBron James left Miami to sign with Cleveland. The 10-time All-Star had played for the Cavs from 2003 to 2010.

Irving and James formed a powerful duo. But they soon formed a "Big Three" when the Cavs traded for forward Kevin Love.

Irving, *right*, and LeBron James, *left*, formed two of the Big Three that led Cleveland back to the playoffs.

FAST FACT

In July 2014, Irving signed a $90 million contract extension lasting through the 2019-20 season.

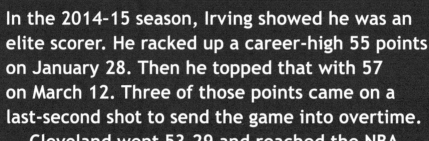

In the 2014-15 season, Irving showed he was an elite scorer. He racked up a career-high 55 points on January 28. Then he topped that with 57 on March 12. Three of those points came on a last-second shot to send the game into overtime.

Cleveland went 53-29 and reached the NBA Finals. Irving scored 30 points in his first career playoff game. But a knee injury ended his season in Game 1 of the Finals.

Irving drives to the hoop in the first half of his 57-point game against San Antonio in 2015.

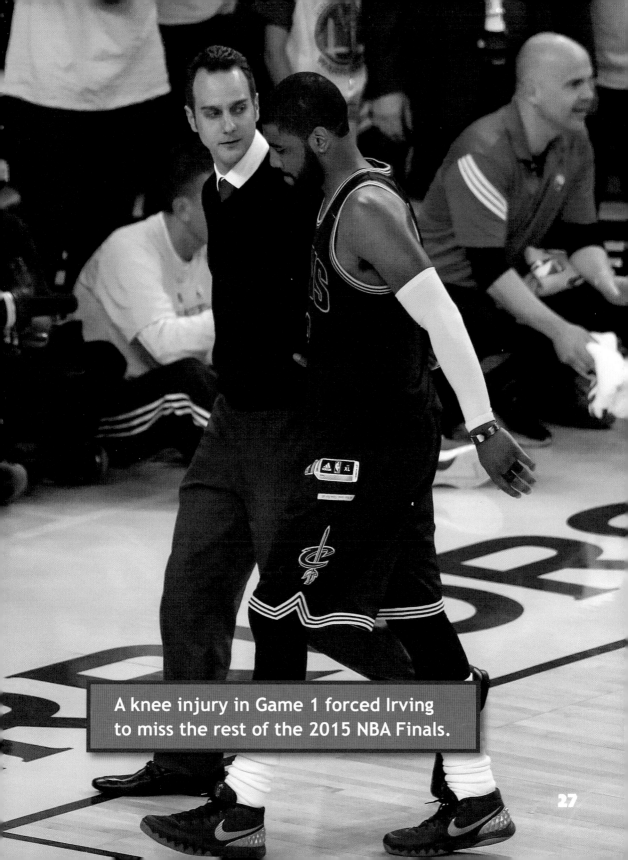

A knee injury in Game 1 forced Irving to miss the rest of the 2015 NBA Finals.

Irving's injury caused him to miss the start of the next season. When he came back, he helped the Cavs to a 57-25 record. They faced Detroit in the first round of the playoffs. Irving scored 31 points in Game 1 and again in Game 4. Cleveland swept Detroit in four games.

Irving made it back to the Finals for a rematch with the Warriors. His last-minute three-pointer in Game 7 gave the Cavaliers the boost they needed to win the title. It was one of the greatest moments in Cleveland sports history. With James, Love, and Irving leading the way, fans hope there are more great moments to come.

Irving goes up for a shot while playing with Team USA at the 2016 Summer Olympics.

FAST FACT

In 2016, Irving became the fourth American player ever to win an NBA title and Olympic gold medal in the same year.

TIMELINE

1992
Kyrie Irving is born on March 23 in Melbourne, Australia.

2011
Irving scores 28 points in his final game with Duke, a March 24 loss to Arizona in the NCAA tournament.

2011
On June 23, the Cleveland Cavaliers select Irving first overall in the 2011 NBA Draft.

2012
Irving scores 34 points in the Rising Stars Challenge at NBA All-Star Weekend on February 24.

2012
On May 15, Irving is named NBA Rookie of the Year. He averages 18.5 points and 5.4 assists per game in his first season.

2013
Irving excels in NBA All-Star Weekend events February 15-17 and plays in his first All-Star Game.

2015
On March 12, Irving scores a team-record and career-high 57 points in Cleveland's overtime win at San Antonio.

2016
Irving makes a go-ahead three-pointer with 53 seconds left to lead the Cavaliers past Golden State for their first NBA title.

GLOSSARY

ARENA
An indoor stadium used for a variety of sports like basketball and hockey.

ASSIST
A pass that leads directly to a scored basket.

CONTRACT
An agreement to play for a certain team.

FRESHMAN
A first-year student.

OVERTIME
An extra period or periods played in the event of a tie.

ROOKIE
A first-year player.

SOPHOMORE
A second-year student.

SWEPT
When a team loses every game in a series.

INDEX

ABOUT THE AUTHOR

Matt Tustison is a sports copy editor at the *Washington Post*.
He also has worked as an editor and writer of children's sports
books for Red Line Editorial.

JB IRVING

Tustison, Matt, 1978–

Kyrie Irving

APR 2 1 2017